Many people call Rosa Parks the "Mother of the Civil Rights Movement."

Rosa Parks grew up in a time when African Americans were treated unfairly. But then Rosa changed history. She stood up for her **civil rights**. And she did it by sitting down! This is her story.

African Americans were called "colored" because of the color of their skin. Signs told them where they could and could not go.

Rosa was born in Alabama in 1913. At that time, there were laws in the South to **segregate** African Americans from white people. This meant that they could not go to the same places, such as restaurants and waiting rooms.

More than 50 students crowded into Rosa's schoolroom each day.

African-American children could not go to the same schools as white children. Rosa's school was for African Americans. It had just one room. It was open only five months a year.

Rosa and Raymond worked with the National Association for the Advancement of Colored People.

Rosa knew that these laws were unfair. In 1931, she met a man named Raymond Parks. He belonged to a group that was working to change the laws. Rosa and Raymond got married. Rosa joined the group, too.

On the bus, African Americans had to follow certain rules that white people did not.

Rosa worked at a store in Montgomery, Alabama. Every day she rode the bus to work. There were unfair laws on the bus, too. The white section was at the front of the bus. The African-American section was at the back.

African Americans could ride in the middle of the bus. But they had to move if white people needed the seats.

December 1, 1955, started like any other day. Rosa went to work at the store. After work she got on the bus to go home. She paid for the ride and sat down in the middle row of seats.

After a few stops, more white people got on the bus. Soon the white section was full. The bus driver asked Rosa to get up and move to the back.

People thought Rosa would not get up because she was tired. But Rosa said she was only "tired of giving in."

Rosa said, "No."
The bus driver said, "I'm going to have you **arrested**."
But Rosa still would not stand up.
The police came and took Rosa to jail.

Many African Americans watched as Rosa went inside to her trial.

Rosa's **trial** was on December 5. That day, many African Americans in Montgomery showed they were on Rosa's side. They would not ride the bus. This is called a **boycott**.

When African Americans stopped riding, the bus company lost a lot of money.

Rosa did not win at the trial. But she did not give up. Neither did other African Americans. Almost all of them stayed off the buses. They found other ways to travel. The boycott lasted 381 days.

When the law was changed, Rosa was photographed riding in the front of the bus. Her story made news around the world.

At last, the **Supreme Court** made a decision. It said that all people who rode the bus had the right to sit where they wanted.

Rosa joined the March on Washington in 1963. It was the biggest civil rights march in history.

But Rosa's work was far from over.
She spoke to people all over the country.
She went on marches for civil rights.
Finally, in 1964, a new law was passed.
It said that all people had to be
treated **equally**.

A street in Montgomery was later named Rosa Parks Boulevard. This was the street where Rosa had ridden the bus.

Rosa Parks received many awards for her courage and her work. She was given our country's Gold Medal of Honor. But her greatest reward was the gift of freedom that she helped give to all people.

This timeline shows some important events in Rosa Parks's life.

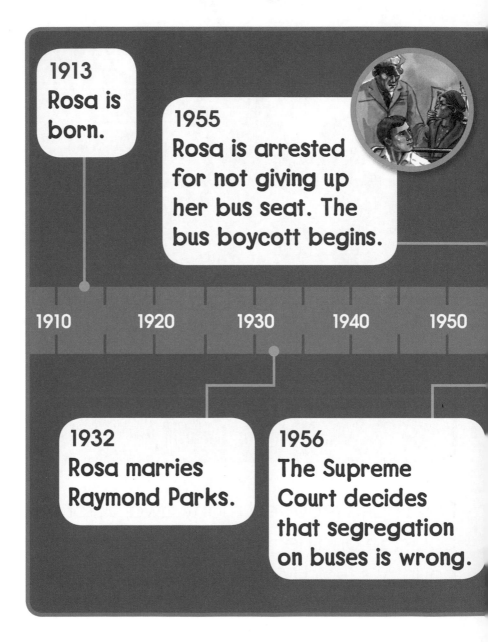

1913
Rosa is born.

1955
Rosa is arrested for not giving up her bus seat. The bus boycott begins.

1910   1920   1930   1940   1950

1932
Rosa marries Raymond Parks.

1956
The Supreme Court decides that segregation on buses is wrong.

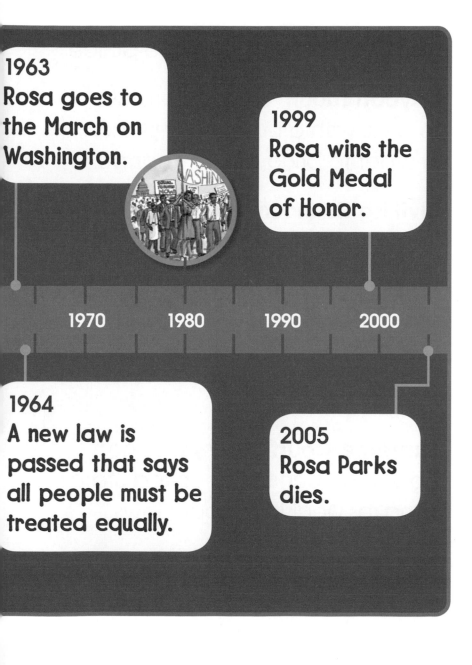

1963
Rosa goes to the March on Washington.

1999
Rosa wins the Gold Medal of Honor.

1970   1980   1990   2000

1964
A new law is passed that says all people must be treated equally.

2005
Rosa Parks dies.

Glossary

arrested (verb) held by the police

boycott (noun) a group's refusal to deal with a business or person, in order to bring about change

civil rights (noun) the rights to have freedom and be treated equally

equally (adverb) in the same way as someone else

segregate (verb) to separate; to keep apart

Supreme Court (noun) the most powerful court in the United States. It makes decisions about laws.

trial (noun) the process of looking at facts in court